Social Letters

Written by
Arun Sagar 'Anand'

Translated by
Editorial Board

V&S PUBLISHERS

Published by:

V&S PUBLISHERS

F-2/16, Ansari road, Daryaganj, New Delhi-110002
☎ 23240026, 23240027 • *Fax:* 011-23240028
Email: info@vspublishers.com • *Website:* www.vspublishers.com

Regional Office : Hyderabad
5-1-707/1, Brij Bhawan (Beside Central Bank of India Lane)
Bank Street, Koti, Hyderabad - 500 095
☎ 040-24737290
E-mail: vspublishershyd@gmail.com

Branch Office : Mumbai
Jaywant Industrial Estate, 2nd Floor–222, Tardeo Road
Opposite Sobo Central Mall, Mumbai – 400 034
☎ 022-23510736
E-mail: vspublishersmum@gmail.com

Follow us on:

All books available at **www.vspublishers.com**

© **Copyright:** *V&S PUBLISHERS*
Edition 2017

Publisher's Note

It gives us pleasure to publish this book on letter writing named **Social Letter**. It had been our cherished desire to bring out a book on letter writing for readers in a systematic and scientific manner.

This book attempts to present rules for letter writing in all possible situations and circumstances. Despite the availability of e-mails, telephones, mobile phones, instant messaging, etc., it is ultimately the correspondence made through letters that matters; whether it is an issue concerning, social, ties. Letters have retained their preponderance in a milieu of communications the way books have remained strong among all readable materials – whether available in printed or digital forms.

Using words in simple and day-to-day language, this book tries to exemplify every kind of letters ordinarily people take recourse to while writing on social subject.

This book, **Social Letters** is presumed to be completed within 30 days. All that is needed by a diligent reader is to devote time to comprehend a few pages each single day and then practise its usage. Ample examples have been given to simplify the process of learning.

We sincerely hope the readers would make the best use of this book to master the art and science of letter writing in all situations and circumstances.

Preface

Innumerable means are available that facilitate communications between two individuals or businesses. New technologies are coming up every other day that expand the sphere of communicating one"s thoughts and ideas. Despite the ease with which telephones and e-mails have made their way into our lives, the uninterrupted run of letter writing continues to flourish. The art of writing has not lost its significance one bit; the way printed books continue with their monopoly in all reading materials. Radios and TVs are just but a small diversion.

It is difficult to fathom the importance of the letter and of its writing. The letter plays a second part only to conversation and to personal contact. Because of the letter no one remains a stranger, and to the letter writer no part of the civilized world is inaccessible. New forms of communication have come up but they all remain the same in essence – conveying an idea or two.

The letter connects persons, and is the vehicle of the progress of humankind. While neither the writer of this book, nor anyone else, can teach by printed page, or orally, the great science or art of letter writing, it is hoped that the contents of this book will be of at least indirect assistance to everyone who uses the mails, and 'every one" includes the whole world.

This book uses simple and everyday language to tell readers the correct way and polished manners to write personal, commercial, business and official letters on all occasions.

A number of model examples have been included to write skilfully individual, personal, family, social and business letters besides others forms of communications written for specific needs - jobs, banking, insurance, e-mails, etc. The examples are intended to help readers to learn the basics and master the science of perfect letter writing. Manner of writing official letters have been extensively given, such as, notification, oath, declaration, press communiqué, press note, ordinance, tender, auction, notice, government official letters, memo and sanction letters.

The book is to be used as a guide so that the reader develops a succinct way of writing high quality letters. I hope that by making the best use of this book not only the ones associated with writing official and other kinds of letters, even the private sector employees, housewives and other interested people would start writing impressive and attractive letters efficiently and easily.

I look forward to suggestions and criticisms for making the forthcoming edition of the book more useful.

– Arun Sagar 'Anand"

Contents

1

Letter Writing

Letter writing has become an important component in social life. The world appears to be interconnected by one way or another. No one has the time to meet another person as much as one would wish.

Letter writing is as old as humanity. Pigeons were used to carry messages in early times. There existed no postal facility then. Things moved on but what didn"t change course was the means of letter writing.

A person can continue to be in touch with another person, wherever he may be, by means of letters. Psychological studies reveal that:

❑ A person wants to preserve whatever he things or visualizes. He wants to share this with someone close. This he can do by means of communicating through letter writing.

❑ People who have spent years in jail reveal that but for maintaining touch with friends and relatives by letter writing, their thought processes, which is alive and kicking, would have dried up long ago.

❑ Pandit Jawaharlal Nehru"s letters to his daughter Indira Gandhi has become historical in true sense. Its relevance is for the posterity. That"s one reason why letters of great people are compiled for the benefit of the coming generations. Letters written by Lenin, Churchill, Mussolini, Napoleon, Hitler and Abraham Lincoln have made them immortal.

❑ Letter writing protects one from excitement, emotions, anger, etc. It is said that Abraham Lincoln used to start writing letters whenever angry. He would download his anger using the means of letter writing. Such letters he would always, instead of sending to the intended recipient, read and reread later to analyse what made him angry in the first place.

❑ If a person talks about his pain, ordinarily others wouldn"t pay much attention. Instead, they would act out the 'sympathy" part. No real feelings. But when the same pain is put down in writing, others try to understand the underlying idea behind the anguish and work out ways to help out.

❑ Letters strengthen the bonds among people. Pen-friendship is a testimony to this fact. People across the world can learn about one another. This helps strengthen cultural and social ties.

Letter writing is a reflection of times. A letter written today may have words like mobile phone, computer, television, google, facebook, internet, etc. We can, similarly, know about the history or geography of one country or another. Dress habits, culture, etc. get mirrored through letters.

Mentioned below are a few points we must take into consideration while writing:

- ❑ Nothing should be written that may compromise the social harmony.
- ❑ Letters must keep one another"s interest in mind.
- ❑ Letters should focus primarily on human welfare and not politics.
- ❑ Nothing irrelevant should find space in a letter.
- ❑ The language used should be easy and simple.
- ❑ A letter should reflect honesty; not hypocrisy.
- ❑ A letter should be brief and to the point.

2

Letter Writing: An Art

Letter writing has a bearing on our personal and social life. They reflect the way we conduct ourselves in society. To know a person, reading a few letters written by him is enough. Letters would reveal the working and thought process of his mind at different times in different situations. The letters symbolise the psychology, emotions, sense of belongings, personal relations and social equations, a person maintains.

A person has become a combination of various pulls and pressures. This finds expression though correspondence. Without letters or other modes of communications, it is difficult to maintain equilibrium in friendship, relations, social mores, work culture, business, polity, etc. The success and failure in life also depends a great deal upon our methods of correspondence. The more successful one is in letter writing, the more successful he is likely to become in future.

The habit of letter writing starts developing right from the student life. Such letters are written to parents, teachers and friends. These reflect the bonds of emotional attachment.

As soon as one enters the adult life, the letters acquire the edge of love, feelings and attachment.

Where personal relations are concerned, letters mostly portray closeness and empathy.

If you want to become a prolific letter writer, please pay attention to the following:

❑ Letter should be logical, short, crisp and clear.

❑ The presentation should be scientific, not full of emotions. Official and managerial letters should be built around solid matters, straightforward and to the point.

❑ The letter should be developed around proper reference and context. It must be clear, else confusion may arise. Before dispatching a letter, one should read it as if the receiver is reading it. Check everything is clear and accurate. If not, make changes where necessary.

❑ Never write a letter when angry.

❑ Always take care of your goodwill.

❑ A letter should be balanced, short and precise.

3

Before Beginning to Write a Letter

A letter is an image of the writer, his attitude, his personality. A letter is talk upon paper; but it is not as easy to write as it is to tell your story in spoken words, because when you talk, your audience is before you, and you can better adapt your words to the receiver who is present, than to one who is absent. If what you say when you talk is not right, and does not have the desired effect, you are likely to have opportunity to explain. What you say in a letter, however, must stand as it is, and is not subject to immediate correction, change or even a 'retake" much like we have in films. Therefore, the letter must be prepared with more care, and with more attention to detail, than is necessary for the spoken word.

It has been said, and with much truth, that nobody can write a letter, or any document, which is guaranteed to be fully and correctly understood by its receiver. The letter writer, therefore, must do his best, for the more care he gives to his letter, the greater likelihood there is of its being properly interpreted by its receiver.

Perfection is impossible, but there is a vast difference between a carelessly thrown-together letter and one which is intelligently written. A large part of the business of the world is conducted by correspondence; and no one can maintain his position without the writing of social letters.

While this book attempts to present rules for letter writing, it must be admitted that outside of the fundamental principles, it is difficult to instruct any one so that he may become, by these instructions alone, a prolific letter writer. Individual judgement and common sense play important parts upon the stage of letter writing. One may be helped by suggestions, and even by rules; but instruction alone is not sufficient. He must put himself into his letters. Proficiency exists only when one realizes their importance, and lets each experience aid him in producing better results. The book doesn"t aim to present more than a few forms of the body of a letter, because such arbitrary examples would be of little use to any proficient letter writer; and the indifferent one, using them, would make his letters framed and confined. One should, then, become familiar with suitable forms, and should adapt them to his conditions, but should not copy verbatim the style or wording of this book or any other for that matter.

A letter writer must keep the following in mind:

Clarity

A letter writer should be clear about the subject matter of the letter. It should be in plain and simple language so that the reader immediately gets to the bottom of the content. Confusion should be avoided at all costs.

Fullness/Absoluteness

Not only a letter should be clear in explaining things, but it should be complete as well. Nothing should be written that is out of context, nor any topic should be repeated. If something comes to mind after the letter has been written, then P.S.(Post Script) written below the letter serves the purpose. The subject missed out of the main letter is mentioned in P.S.

Ease

Simplicity is the lifeblood of any letter. It must be written with ease and appear logical moving from one idea to another. Difficult words have to be avoided. Small and short sentences make a letter easy to understand.

In Short

Brevity is the soul of a letter. It should also be complete in all respects without missing out on anything relevant. Unnecessary verbosity mars the ease in understanding the text matter.

Effective

Words must be used with care and caution. Only popular words and in current usage convey the meaning to an average reader. Letter should be interesting so that the recipient finds it interesting to read.

Manners

Language used should be polite and full of respect and etiquette. Courtesy breeds courtesy. Correct salutations make for a prompt reply. This fact must not be overlooked under any circumstances.

Attractive

Appearance of a letter enhances its attraction, makes it more readable, and sub-consciously forces the reader to take note of the contents. The language of the letter deserves careful attention. Name and address should be written with accurately. No one likes to see his name misspelt.

Paper

A good quality paper draws the attention of the reader and makes for a good impression. Whereas students tend to use colourful and fancy papers, the grown-ups go for good quality plain papers. Ordinary papers are good enough for day-to-day mails; light-weight papers should be preferred for air mails. This reduces the expenses on postage.

Pen & Ink

Coloured inks, other than blue or black, should be used only during special occasions. Coloured inks don"t find approval from most people.

Writing with a pencil is a big No, while writing a letter. They become difficult to read or make out. *Therefore, every letter should be written with a pen.*

Accuracy & Cleanliness

Every sentence must be complete and carry a definite meaning. It should be easy to read and understand. While writing a business letter, special care must be taken regarding a bill, *hundi*, book of accounts, other commercial details, failing which the goodwill of the firm may be compromised.

Satisfactory

The credibility of a business letter hinges on the clarity and completeness with regard to details. Confusion at all costs should be avoided. The letter must clearly mention the weight, price, type, quality, amount and discount regarding the product. Making a mention of the available guarantee increases the value of the product and enhances the image of the firm.

Systematic

Points raised in the letter should follow an established sequence. Only one issue should be mentioned under a single point. Long sentences must be avoided. The letter, if necessary, should be made attractive by going in for an additional paragraph.

At Proper Time

Delay hurts a business and its growth. It hits the image of the firm as well. Letters should be promptly replied. If it is not possible to reply with sought-after information, an acknowledgement of the letter must be sent. Make a point to apologise, if for any reason, reply couldn"t be made in time.

Planning

A letter should be properly planned before writing. *Clarity is of utmost importance.* The reader must comprehend the subject matter of the letter. Respectful and polite words make the reader favourably inclined towards the writer.

Writing

A letter reflects the personality of the writer. Hence, it is important for a writer to be careful in the choice of words or sentences.

A letter may give out the establishment and line of organization, a writer has in his work ethics. *Good style and polished manners leave a sound impression on the recipient.*

Envelope

An envelope should be carefully chosen, capable of reflecting the image of the sender. The name of the recipient should begin close to the centre of the envelope and about one inch below the top edge. It should be followed by C/O (where required). This should be followed by House No, Lane, Locality, Name of the town/city, PIN Code, etc.

We can write Mr/Mrs/Sri/Smt, etc. before the name of a gentleman/lady. 'Esq" is often written before the name of any distinguished person. For an unmarried girl, the term, 'Miss" is used. Whereas 'To" is written in English, the term, 'Sewa Men" is used in Hindi.

Beginning to Write a Letter

While writing a letter, the writer should mention his 'address" on the top right hand side of the paper. This is followed by the 'date" right below the address. If the address is already printed on the paper, there is no need to write the address afresh. The name and address of the recipient is written on the left side of the paper. The form of writing is mainly used in business correspondence. It facilitates the office clerk to enter the sender"s and recipient"s address in the dispatch register. However, in personal letters, the address of the recipient is not written.

Subject of the Letter

There is little point elaborating at this stage on the subject matter of a letter. This is fully explained in subsequent chapters. It is enough to understand that it is the 'subject" that necessitates writing of any letter. The subject is the reason for entering into any correspondence. We have compiled a series of letters in the following pages taking note of various circumstances that directly or indirectly suggest us to write a letter. The readers would be able to understand the manner and presentation of writing letters in the most appropriate and modern style.

Correct Style of Writing

The writer must choose words with care. A word wrongly used could change the meaning of the letter altogether. The meaning of the letter may become confusing or even irrelevant. The words that convey the intended meaning should only be used.

Similarly, the writer should pay attention to the *accuracy of the words also.* Correct spellings of the words are important. Unlike spoken words, there is no chance to recall the word that has been put down. The letter will stay as it is, wrong words, unintended words or confusing words. You can"t wish them away. Therefore, be careful while using any word.

Use of Comma

Sometimes placing a 'comma" at a wrong place can change the meaning of the sentence. You wanted to convey one thing but by placing the 'comma" at a wrong place, the idea gets changed. In fact, even the opposite meaning could also be conjured up. The writer must put a full stop after completion of a sentence. An explanatory sign is marked as ('!"). While quoting someone else"s sentence, inverted comma ('…") is indicated. Mark of interrogation ('?") is used whenever the sentence asks for an answer.

Typing Letters

Some opine that personal letters shouldn"t be typed. Intimacy is lost and formality is introduced. But many people have started sending personal letters duly typed. The advantage typed letters introduce is ease in reading and simplicity in capturing the theme.

Business Letters

The major difference between success and failure of a business is attributed to the way correspondence is done. *Writing business letters is a great art.* It is considered important to make correspondence in a timely manner; and without delay. Business letters are divided into following five sections:

1. Sales-related correspondence
2. Day-to-day regular correspondence
3. Accounts-related correspondence
4. Advertisement-related correspondence
5. Establishment-related correspondence

The above mentioned letters can be sub-divided into many other sections. Irrespective of sections or sub-sections, every correspondence ultimately ends up contributing to sales. No letter should be delayed in responding quickly, more so a business one. *A prompt reply boosts a firm"s image.* Moreover, it is a matter of courtesy and business ethics.

Business letters should preferably be typed. Many large organisations make use of a shorthand writer to dictate letters for eventual typing.

Closing a Letter

Whereas in English language, letters written in the first person close with the words, 'Yours Truly" or 'Yours faithfully", the corresponding Hindi words are 'Aapka" or 'Tumhara". 'Aapka" is used only as a mark of respect for an elder person. Form of closing a letter requires more care and attention in business letters than in personal ones.

Business Signature

Business letters should be signed such that the recipient finds practically no difficulty in deciphering his name. If the writing is illegible, his name should be clearly typed below the signature.

Goodwill of the Firm

An attractive manner of letter writing impresses the recipient and enhances the goodwill of the firm. Care must be taken to see that the image of the firm gets a leg-up with every correspondence.

4
Letter Writing and its Importance

Letter writing is a process of exchanging communications by means of letters. It could be between two firms, organisations, customers, or personal relations. It could be between a firm and a customer. In fact, any exchange of ideas between two individuals or entities is broadly classified as *correspondence through letters.*

Importance of Letter Writing

Letters are an important form of communication. It is a medium to exchange views. Following points constitute the major components of letter writing:

❑ **Written medium of expression** – Letter is a medium of exchange of ideas between two letter writers. It can be resorted to when inconvenience is experienced while making any oral communication.

❑ **Simplicity in record keeping** – It is difficult to keep a record of oral discussions. But a written communication can be conveniently filed for future reference. It can be gone through as and when required.

❑ **Opportune time to use considered thoughts** – It sometimes happens that we speak something that we never intended to say. But a letter writer saves himself from such undesirable situations. If a word has been erroneously written, it can always be amended, modified and reset for improved impression.

❑ **Continuity in relationship** – Letters help in cementing the relationship between two persons or firms even if they are not meeting each other on a regular basis.

❑ **As a representative** – *A letter in essence is a representative of the writer.* While a personal letter represents an individual, a business letter does the same for an organisation.

❑ **As a medium of complaint** – *A complaint made orally is not as effective as a written one.* A written one stands testimony to the proof that some difficulty or inconvenience is experienced against which redressal has been sought. It forms part of a complaint register.

❑ **Conveyor of pleasure and pain** – A letter is a communication that can convey good news or an inconvenient one. It acts as a postman who can bring in news of all sorts – good, bad or ugly.

❑ **Government"s messages** – The government circulates its orders, information, news, etc. through the medium of letters.

- **Proof** – The letters stand proof of a document circulated or conveyed.

- **As a literature** – Writers write books, notes, novels, poems, etc. and place before the general public for recreation, or information or enjoyment. This eliminates the sense of loneliness.

- **As a social reformer** – Various newspapers and magazines earmark space for people to write their views, comments or complaints against the ills existing in the society. The columns represent both, the bouquets and the brickbats.

- **As a critic** – Letters are means of critical appreciation written by a reader of any literary work or happening of common public importance.

- **Economic medium** – In these days of busy life, letters are a very economical medium to remain in touch with family, friends and relatives. They are equally useful in maintaining business relationships.

Social Correspondence

Letters that demand spreading of awareness to check and to put an end to prevalent issues adversely affecting the society are covered under the head, 'social correspondence". Intercaste marriages, marriage dissolutions, or female foeticides are some of the issues that immediately necessitate intervention and action. A few examples are given below:

(Sample-1)

Name and address of the sender
Dated:

Sri Devesh Choudhary
President, Zila Panchayat
Naharpur

Sub: About Intercaste Marriages

Dear Chaudharyji,

It has come to my notice that you are organizing a social meet in the coming month. We observe that the intercaste marriagess are gaining ground in the society quite rapidly. Therefore, please do not bring forward any resolution that condemns and punishes such marriages. I do agree that intercaste marriages sometimes let-in havoc in the lives of girls. Currently, the girls are not literate enough to easily take to such marriages on their own. It is mostly the boys who are taking the initiative. Therefore, to think about banning this kind of tying the nuptial knot will generate discord within the families.

It would be worthwhile creating educational opportunities for girls. The best course is to make them as qualified as boys. This would enable them to take a conscious decision in matters of selecting a suitable companion for themselves. There is no alternative to taking such a course of action.

I am writing this to apprise you with my views since I would be out of town; and am in no position to attend the meet.

Yours sincerely,
Gaurav Garg

(Sample-2)
Suggestion for Prevention of Divorce

Dear Radhika,

I have received your letter yesterday. I feel greatly perturbed that your relations with Rajiv have sunk to such an extent that you are considering the option of divorce. Are you left with no option? Is divorce the only choice left? Would you gain anything from dissolution? By the way, is there someone else in your life ready to tie the knot?

I still think Rajiv is a nice person. I may be wrong but I feel there is some kind of ego clash between you two. While I am not for woman always bending backwards to accommodate, nevertheless, I see no harm in trying to find a middle ground. Moreover, there is a child to be looked after, so please give compromise a go.

Look around, you will find our culture and societal norms provide stability to marriages. We ourselves have literally fought over many times; and shortly afterwards, came to our original selves. Disagreements between a husband and wife are a phenomenon that happens off and on and every time it occurs, the word, 'divorce" shouldn"t cross our minds.

I sincerely hope you will consider my views in the right spirit. Divorce is no solution; rather it creates more problems – both personal and social. If you are in a state of anger, think about it some other time. But give it a sincere and serious thought on this vital issue. You would find there is a valid reason to stay together.

Please write to me with a cool head.

Your friend,
Navneet Parihar

(Sample-3)
Suggestion to an Editor

Dear Arvind,

Your daily newspaper is coming under increasing influence of English words these days. Despite you being an editor, this rising tendency gives me jitters, an uncomfortable feeling. Hindi words – even the popular ones – are being replaced with English ones for no rhyme or reason. What was the great idea to substitute 'Vishvavidyalaya" with 'University"? There are many words whose substitution is just not required. I think, as an editor, it is your moral duty to diffuse this tendency, or nip this practice.

I am fully aware of the preference of the owners to run the newspaper purely in the manner they decide and if employment is to continue, editors have to succumb to their policies. This is not the correct perspective. You can, at least, offer your viewpoint. Newspapers carry a responsibility to march forward the cultural mores and also to reinforce cementing the social traditions.

More or less identical policy of 'encouraging English" is being sought to be implemented in our newspaper, but I have been successful in resisting thus far. If forced to decide one way or the other, don"t you think it would be a good idea to form an organisation and start a newspaper of our own? Do you have any idea, suggestion, etc?

Looking forward to your considered views on all these issues!

Yours sincerely,
Avinash
Sandhya Dainik

(Sample-4)
Social Invitation

Ms. Anita Aggarwal
Secretary, Stri Samaj
Kurla, Mumbai

Dear Sister,

I feel pleased that you have become secretary of the *Stri Samaj* of Kurla. Law and order situation in Mumbai has deteriorated to a great extent. I am calling a meeting of Mumbai, *Stri Samaj*. Time has come when women need to protect themselves. My wish is to have such women"s security bodies is every nook and corner. Major problem is that unsocial elements try to get friendly with women, pass vulgar and lewd remarks and otherwise become a nuisance to them. Incidence of rape is on the rise. Poor girls are lured into marriage only to be sold later on. Young girls are being trafficked. Government agencies are practically helpless before mafia indulging in such activities. Political leaders worry for nothing except remembering you at the time of elections. Women are the worst sufferer of this attitude. There is a meeting organised on 13th July, 2013. Please arrange to reach the *Stri Bhawan* at Dadar at 2:00 pm.

Yours sincerely,
Kamna Achrekar
Secretary
Brihad Stri Samaj, Mumbai

Letters of Complaint

No one is pleased complaining. When a person gets tired of seeking resolution to some issue and the concerned officials just don"t take notice, the complainant decides to take things forward to higher authorities to press for necessary grievance or removal or corrective action. Such letters are termed as *complaint letters.* Examples of complaints are, non-receipt of money orders, registered letters, telegrams, gas connection, non-servicing of telephones, theft, indecent behaviour of bus conductors, railway staff, etc. Failure of cleanliness of common areas, such as, garbage pile up, upkeep of roads, failure to maintain regular power supplies, water supplies, diverting supplies meant for public distribution into open markets, careless attitude of civic employees, etc., come under the same heading. Resorting to public complaints should be backed with solid evidences.

(Sample-1)

[Personal]

Non-delivery of Money Order

Name and address of the sender
Dated:

In charge, Post Office
Gopal Mandir Post Office
Chattri Chowk
Ujjain (M.P.)

Sub: Non-delivery of Money Order

Dear Sir,

I had sent from this post office a money order for ₹ 4,000/- addressed to my father at Bhawanipur.

This morning my father informed me that the said money order has not reached him till now.

My mother was to undergo an eye surgery at the Jiwan Nursing Home during the last month. Unfortunately, for want of money, the operation couldn"t be carried out. A number of visits to the post office there elicited no response from the staff saying that no such money order ever arrived.

Due to sheer indifference of the post office staff, my family had to suffer undue hardships. Will these people be able to visualise the difficulties imposed on them for no fault of theirs?

I request you to kindly look into the matter seriously and help deliver the money promptly. I have enclosed a copy of the money order receipt for your reference.

Thanking you,

Yours faithfully,
Anurag Sharma

(Sample-2)
Unbecoming Behaviour of the Bus Conductor

Name and address of the sender
Dated:

The Manager
Maharashtra State Road Transport Corporation
Thane

Sub: Unbecoming Conduct of the Bus Conductor

Dear Sir,

I wish to draw your kind attention to the unbecoming conduct of the Ramnagar Depot, bus conductor. Last 20th November, I travelled with my family from Narayanpur to Ramnagar Depot on bus no-M10 Q4572.

The fare from Narayanpur to Ramnagar is ₹ 10/- and therefore, for six persons it comes to ₹ 60/-. I gave him a ₹ 100/- note and expected the balance amount to be paid back. Saying that he would refund later when he gets it, the conductor moved forward to collect fares from other passengers. When we reached near our destination, I reminded him but to no avail. He evaded me under the pretext of not having the required change. We had to finally get down at Ramnagar without getting the due amount of ₹ 40/-

The badge number of the conductor is 6734.

I request you to take note of the above incident and initiate necessary action so that the said conductor refrains from acting likewise in future.

Thanking you,

Yours faithfully,
Kulvant Shinde

(Sample-3)
Non-functional Telephone

Name and address of the sender
Dated:

The Zonal Manager
MTNL
Kalatalab
Kalyan (Maharashtra)

Sub: Telephone No-23768549 – Not Working

Dear Sir,

    I reside in Bhim Nagar locality within Kalyan Telecom Zone. For the past 15 days, my telephone no- 23768549 is practically dead. I had lodged a complaint on 15th of this month but to no avail. The token number is 347. When enquired a few days back, the fault was attributed to the underground cable wiring. Had it been so, the telephones of my neighbours wouldn"t have started functioning. They too were told about the fault in cable.

    Clearly, the fault is not been attended to with any seriousness. My father is a heart patient. We may need the services of a telephone any moment.

    I request you to depute your linemen at the earliest so that the telephone instrument is set right promptly.

    Thanking you,

Yours faithfully,
Ajit Pawar

(Sample-4)

Irregularities in the Supply of Gas Cylinders

Name and address of the sender

Dated:

The Manager
Baldev Gas Agency
Bhav Nagar (Gujarat)

Sub: Irregularities in the Supply of Gas Cylinders

Dear Sir,

The consumer number of my gas cylinder connection is 5674. Three weeks back, I had requisitioned your office for a refill cylinder. I regret to inform you that despite 20 days having elapsed, no refill is in sight. It is but common knowledge that your line staff ensures prompt delivery of refills to those willing to pay ₹ 20-25 to them by way of extraneous consideration. Others are doled out some innate and frivolous replies. An honest consumer has to wait at least 15 to 20 days before he gets supply. The hardship we have to suffer is untold. The attitude the linesmen bear is simply one of indifference.

I request you to take note of the above, investigate the matter and issue strict instructions for timely and regular delivery of refills.

Thanking you,

Yours faithfully,

Dilip Kulkarni

(Sample-5)
Complaint to Railway Authorities
Aronima Textiles

Address:
Date:......

The Chief Commercial Manager
Central Railway
Kalyan

Sir,

Yesterday we secured the delivery of four bundles of Banarasi saris sent by the Kamal Textiles, Varanasi wide goods receipt no.......... Date...........However, the packing of one of the bundles was found broken. The matter has been duly reported to the Assistant Station Master, Kalyan. As per the bill, each bundle contained 100 Banarasi saris. While the three bundles correctly had 100 saris as mentioned, the bundles with broken seals contained only 96 saris. The pilferage of 4 saris amount to a loss of ₹ 8000/- to us for railways are fully responsible. For your perusal, we are enclosing the bill as received by us. You will get to know the cost of each sari. We request you to conduct suitable enquiry and compensate us for the loss caused in this transaction.

Thanking you,

Yours faithfully,
Name

(Sample-6)
Complaint Regarding Damaged Product
Jagan Furniture

Address:
Date:

M/S Omega Furniture
20, Furniture Bazaar
Ulahas Nagar

Sir,

We are in receipt of the parcel sent by you on dated. On opening the parcel, we discovered that five showcases and three dressing case had their glasses broken or damaged. Further that seven showcases had glass coverings that don"t fit properly. It appears that the fault with the staff at the packing counter. We had shown the damaged showcases and dressing cases to the truck driver. Kindly send an expert to rectify the error; at the earliest.

Thanking you,

Yours faithfully,
Name

(Sample-7)

[Public]

Irregularities in Power Supply

Address:

Date:

The Executive Engineer
Maharashtra State Electricity Board
Shanti Chambers
Vashind – 421601

Sub: Irregularities in Electric Supply

Dear Sir,

  I regret to point out the extremely irregular power supply people of Vashind suffer. The Friday cut-outs regularly but for no apparent reason is a great menace to the locality, as a whole. The power goes off again in the evening and the residents, particularly the students and traders suffer enormously. It"s difficult to sit at home or remain peaceful in the absence of power. Since examinations are at hand, students are a worried lot. We are at a loss of thought and reason as to why the power situation has become so erratic? We request you to look into the matter urgently and set the power supply in houses in order so that the people of Vashind can live a comfortable life.

  Thanking you,

Yours faithfully,

Name

(Sample-8)
Complaint Against Inadequate Water Supply

Address :
Date :

The Commissioner
Ulhasnagar Mahanagar Palika
Ulhasnagar

Sub: Inadequate Water Supply

Sir,

With deep anguish, we, the residents of Gandhi Nagar wish to draw your attention to the huge water scarcity being faced by us for a long time. The speed with which Gandhi Nagar developed has been commendable, but the water supply arrangement didn"t keep pace with it. People suffer acute water problem. Water is supplied once a day for about half an hour and comes with enormous force. But affer that often water taps remain dry for two consecutive days. At times, this leads to quarrel among the residents. For lack of adequate availability of water, the people have to perforce, fetch water from other areas or from boring pumps, which are few and far between. We had hoped that the establishment of Mahanagar Palika will lead to substantial improvement in the living conditions but the situation remains as before. We sincerely hope you will take some concrete positive steps to improve the water supply conditions in Gandhi Nagar.

Thanking you,

Yours faithfully,
(Names & Signatures of
few respectable people)

Date:.........

(Sample-9)
Lethargy of Bank Staff

The Branch Manager
Oriental Bank of Commerce
197, Paschim Vihar
New Delhi – 110063

Sub: Lethargy of Banking Personnel

Sir,

    I wish to inform you that I am quite sick of the attitude of your staff. There are three counters for making payments but two of them almost always remain closed leading to long queues in the lone operating counter. Often employees instead of attending to customers go to their colleague"s desk and start gossiping. There is a board within the bank displaying the schedule of average time taken to perform certain functions, for example a cheque presented for encashment is scheduled to be paid within 20 minutes but in fact, it takes something around 30-40 minutes. Cheques of other banks take 4-5 days for clearing. We request you to kindly instruct your staff suitably so that customers don"t have to face harassment or inconvenience.

    Thanking you,

Yours faithfully,
Name & Address

Dated:...........

Irregularities at Post Office

The Post Master
Dak Bhawan
Sundar Vihar
New Delhi

Sir

We, the residents of Sundar Vihar, are facing a lot of difficulties and lack of facilities at the post office for days on end as the posted materials remain unavailable. If the envelope as the available then the postcards may not. In fact, one or the other is mostly out of stock. Enquiries are rudely replied to. Another problem is the postal boxes are not cleared regularly. A card deposited inside the postal box may remain inside for some days. Dak distribution leaves much to be desired timely and correct delivery to the addressee is not always there. We request you to take suitable steps to remove the grievances of the people living in that area.

Thanking you,

Yours faithfully,
(Residents of Sundar Vihar with
Name, Address & Mobile Number)

Dated:.........

Complaint against Dirt, Filth and Garbage in the Colony

The Sanitation Officer
Uttam Nagar
New Delhi

Sub: Filthy Conditions in the Colony

Sir

    We request to inform you that in the last few months the gutter drains and sewerage systems are not being cleared properly. For lack of effective cleaning, filth and other materials choke the pipes leading to overflow. Dirty water gets into the houses. Sweepers don"t care at all. This leads to flies, mosquitoes and other disease carrying insects flooding the area and its environment. Fumigation is not done regularly to check and control the growth of such disease causing flies and mosquitoes. If things like this goes on any longer, epidemics may erupt. It could also lead to loss of life as well. We request you to kindly pay urgent attention to our pleas to restore proper sanitation in the area.

    Thanking you,

Yours faithfully,
(Residents of Uttam Nagar
With Address & Mobile Number)

Date:..........

Sale of Subsidised Kerosene Oil in the Market

The Rationing Officer
Circle Office
Madipur
Paschim Vihar
New Delhi

Sub: Unauthorised Sale of Kerosene Oil

Sir,

We the residents of Madipur want to inform you that off and on sugar is made available at the ration shop but kerosene oil, never. The shopkeepers complain that kerosene oil has not been supplied and that as and when it comes, delivery would be made. Despite lodging complaint in the register maintained at the shop, no improvement took place. In collusion with unsocial elements, grains, sugar and kerosene oil are being sold in the open market. We request you to look into the matter on an urgent basis and take strict action against the concerned shopkeepers and other colluding elements of the society.

Thanking you,

Yours sincerely,
Residents of Madipur
Name & Mobile Numbers

Date:..........

1

Letters to the Editor

Newspapers and Magazines have a unique place in the society. They reflect the social, economic and political happenings in the society, when writing a letter to the editor (drawing his attention to the improvement of the power situation, cleanliness, news regarding social happenings, etc.) You must mention your name, address and telephone number. If you don"t want your name to appear with the letter, make a request to the editor to this effect but he must have your details.

(Sample-1)
Requesting the Editor to Publish an Article

Address:
Date:

The Editor
Dainik Hindustan
New Delhi

Sir,

I am sending you a poem, *Mera pyara basta* for your perusal with a request to publish the same under the *Bachpan* column in the forthcoming Sunday edition of your esteemed *Dainik Hindustan*. I would be highly obliged for this favour.

Thanking you,

Yours sincerely,
Name & Signature

(Sample-2)

Annual Subscription

Address:

Date:

The Secretary
Sahitya Academy
Ravindra Bhawan, 35 Ferozshah Marg
New Delhi 110001

Dear Sir,

I am sending you by Money Order (MO) a sum of ₹.........towards the annual subscription for *Samkaleen Bhartiya Sahitya*. Please start dispatching the magazine as soon as the remittance reaches you.

Thanking you,

Yours sincerely,
Name & Address

(Sample-3)

News Regarding Fire

The Editor
Lokmat
Mumbai – 400021

Sir,

I have attached a news item on fire in the locality for the favour of publication in your popular newspaper. Kindly do the needful and oblige.

Thanking you,

Yours faithfully,
Name & Signature

Encl: The news item :

Fire Engulfed 50 Houses in the Slum Colony

Last night, a razing fire engulfed the slum colony of Shadipur in New Delhi in which five lives were lost and about 20 grievously injured. According to the fire brigade sources, 50 houses were completely burnt. The fire began around 12 in the midnight and could only be doused in the next one and a half hours. Loss of goods and properties in the fire is estimated to be around ₹ 3 lakhs.

The injured have been admitted to the Ram Manohar Hospital. An enquiry has been ordered to investigate the causes of fire.

(Sample-4)
Dead Body Found

Address:
Dated:

The Editor
Navbharat Times
7, Bahadur Shah Zafar Marg
New Delhi

Sir,

I have enclosed a news item, *Unidentified body found* for publication in your esteemed newspaper. Kindly publish it at the earliest.

Thanking you,

Yours faithfully,
(Name & Signature)

Encl: News item attached :

Unidentified Body Found

A dead body aged between 20 to 25 of a male was found nude in Gandhi Nagar park in East Delhi! The body bore infliction by a sharp weapon on the chest, neck, shoulder, etc. The police believes the removal of clothes from the body was done to hide the identity. The Gandhi Nagar Police was tipped off by an unknown caller informing them of the body. The police took charge of the body and sent it for post-mortem.

(Sample-5)
Truck – Jeep Collision

Address:
Date:

The Editor
Navbharat Times
7 Bahadur Shah Zafar Marg
New Delhi

Sir,

I have enclosed a news item, *Truck – jeep collision* for publication in your esteemed newspaper. Kindly publish the news at a prominent place.

Thanking you,

Yours faithfully,
Name & Signature

Encl: The news item

Truck – Jeep Collision: Two Dead, Four Injured

Last night, there was a head on collision between a truck and a jeep at Mahipalpur on the Gurgaon highway. The impact was so great that the jeep became a rumble of metallic pieces leaving two occupants dead and four injured. The injured were admitted to a government hospital in Mahipalpur. The jeep was on its way from Alwar to Kanpur. The jeep driver, Manohar died on the spot. The truck driver was allegedly under the influence of alcohol and he turned the truck towards Mahipalpur road without giving any signal.

(Sample-6)
A Suggestion Regarding Materials Published in Special Section of Newspapers

Address:
Date:

The Editor
Navbharat Times
Mumbai

Sir,

I am a regular reader of your newspaper. Every week, I anxiously await the *Suruchi* magazine that comes with the newspaper on Sunday. As a matter of fact, *Suruchi* is a storehouse of information. Every article, more so the column named *Hastakshar* is well written. To make *Suruchi*, a little more popular, I have a suggestion if Amritvani and 'Crossword" are also included, *Suruchi* will become lot more better in fact, it would tend to become a full-fledged literary magazine. I hope you will give my suggestion a due consideration.

Thanking you,

Yours faithfully,
Name & Signature

To Check Smoking

Address:
Date:

The Chief Editor
Jansatta
New Delhi

Sir,

The *Jansatta* of 4th November carried a news item informing that a youth below 18 was fined for smoking in Singapore. I hope such a law should be there in India also. You would notice that boys below 18 smoke on the road with gay abandon. It has practically become a fashion. In fact, there is nothing healthy about it at all. It is one of the leading causes of Cancer, Tuberculosis, etc. What is necessary is to have a check on promotions that encourage its use! Mere displaying advertisements on cigarette packs carrying messages of Cancer is not enough. Cigarette sellers around the school and college premises should be moved out at least 500 metres away and if necessary, fined. To inculcate in younger generation a sense of belonging to the nation, 'No Smoking Day" should be celebrated on a fixed date throughout the country.

Thanking you,

Yours faithfully,
Name & Signature

(Sample-8)
Request Not to Display Advertisements in the Middle of a Programme

Address:
Date:

The Editor
Yashobhumi
Mumbai – 400017

Sir,

In recent terms, there is a noticeable increase in time being given for advertisements; especially in the middle of popular programmes and serials broadcasted over the TV. Things have come to such a pass that not just during religion based serials or cricket matches, advertisements are being placed during news also and repeated every now and then.

My suggestion is that if they are to be displayed at all, then they should be slotted at the beginning or at the end of the serial. We hope you will give the suggestions their due.

Thanking you,

Yours faithfully,
Name & Address

(Sample-9)

Misbehaviour of Driver/Conductor of a Bus

Address:

Date:

The Editor
Hindustan
New Delhi – 110001

Dear Sir,

Off and on, we hear of the unbecoming behaviour of bus conductors in public transport. Last week, I experienced this in Delhi"s bus no DL 1P 6483! No sooner the bus started from Sarai Kale Khan Interstate Bus Terminal to Faridabad, then a heated exchange of words took place between a lady passenger and the conductor. The conductor used filthy language. When other passengers objected, the conductor threatened to deboard the lady passenger. When objected again by most of the passengers, the bus had reached Badarpur. There both the driver and the conductor got down from the bus unmindful of the inconvenience caused to the passengers. More than an hour elapsed before the bus started moving again.

The passengers suffered in the sheltering heat for no fault of theirs. Through your newspaper, I want to draw the attention of the senior Delhi Transport Corporation officials to the lack of decency and etiquette among your line staff and give them suitable training that such untoward incidents do not occur in future and if necessary, punish the bad apples amongst them.

Yours faithfully,

Name & Signature

(Sample-10)

On Gambling in the Colonies

Address:
Date:

The Editor
Navbharat Times
7, Bahadur Shah Zafar Marg
New Delhi

Sir,

These days gambling has spread its wings in many colonies. There are secret cells where they are organised. New faces turn up quite often. During the last one month, it appears to have solidified its tentacles. The matter has been reported to the police but the effect is zero. It appears some policemen are in collusion with the gambling operators. Gambling has raised a new question of law and order and security. Frequently, quarrels and fighting breaks out among the gamblers.

This disturbs the peace of the area. We hope you will publish this so that the authorities take necessary action to bring security to the society while acting seriously upon the gambling operators.

Yours faithfully,
Name & Signature

(Sample-11)

Bad Elements, Ruffians in the Society

Address:
Date:

The Editor
Rajasthan Patrika Dainik
Jaipur

Sir,

I want to draw attention towards the rising graph of incidences, such as crime fights, etc. between anti-social elements within the society. Newspapers carry news of goondaism almost every day. The sense of fear has grown among the overage people. Daylight robberies, murder, shootout, looting, molestation, rape, etc. have become almost like a regular news items. Such news have started shaking the conscience of people.

The question is how to get rid of it. Government says police personnels are being deployed in great numbers to stop the rot. Unfortunate outcome is that lawlessness is increasing in direct proportion to the increase in numbers of police personnels. People have a feeling that the police is in hand and glove with the anti-social elements. That"s why they are acquitted when the matter goes to courts.

I wonder what exactly the police is expected to do. Security, protection maintaining peace has gone to dogs. Unfortunately, due to the callousness and indifference of a few police and officers, the entire police department is earning a bad name. We must also recognise that political and bureaucratic interference prevents people from doing their best. Unless this interference is stopped completely, peace won"t visit the society.

I hope you agree with this.

Yours faithfully,
Name & Signature

(Sample-12)
To Prevent Road Accidents

Address:
Date:

The Editor
Jansatta
Mumbai – 400021

Sir,

Through your esteemed newspaper, I want to draw the kind attention of the concerned authorities in the government towards frequent accidents occurring between the Mahatma Gandhi Road and Badlapur Road. Five accidents have taken place on this stretch of road during the last two months. Hospitals, offices and schools lie connected to this important road link. Being a road leading to station this results in continuous flow of traffic vehicles which fly past at a high speed. Absence of footpath leads to great numbers being compelled to walk on the road. Hence, I have a few suggestions to avoid accidents :

❑ Shopkeepers shouldn"t be allowed to park their vehicles on the road and be asked to use proper parking areas.

❑ Cart vendors should be moved away. This in itself would create enough space for pedestrians.

❑ Speed breakers and zebra crossings should be constructed in front of the Saraswati Vidyalaya. The speed limit of 10 km should be imposed on vehicular traffic.

❑ Traffic signals should be erected near the station and those breaking rules should be acted upon promptly.

❑ To allow for unhindered flow during rush hours, the traffic police should be posted at the various sensitive points.

❑ Keeping in mind the increasing vehicular traffic on the Badlapur station area, a subway should be constructed to allow people to reach offices and homes on time.

I appeal to the municipal and traffic authorities to apply the above suggestions in order to prevent further road accidents.

Thanking you,

Yours faithfully,
Name & Signature

(Sample-13)

Adulteration at the Petrol Pump

Address:

Date:

The Editor
Veer Arjun
7, Bahadur Shah Zafar Marg
New Delhi

Dear Sir,

Through your esteemed newspaper, I want to draw the attention of the government towards the activities, such as adulteration at the petrol pump in the Madipur locality. Kindly publish this within the 'complaints column" of your newspaper.

There is a colossal adulteration of kerosene oil in petrol in the Madipur petrol pump which is sold to the public. Unhindered, this is being done by the owners in collusion with authorities from the sales department who get bribed heavily. It is alleged that this nefarious activities is being resorted to on exchange for substantial sums. These government authorities are sucking the hard earned money of gullible public. Moreover, adulterated petrol ends up damaging the engine of the vehicles. The cost of maintenance of the vehicles goup in proportion to the adulterated mix. For want of alternative avenues, people have to perforce depend on this particular petrol pump to refill their tanks.

Taking the above factors into consideration, it is requested that senior authorities should clamp down the dubious activities by taking stringent action on the erring staff.

Thanking you,

Yours faithfully,
Name

(Sample-14)
Dirt, Garbage and Lack of Cleanliness in the Locality

Address:
Date:

The Chief Editor
Navbharat Times
7, Bahadur Shah Zafar Marg
New Delhi

Sir,

    Through the columns of your newspaper, I want to draw the kind attention of the civic authorities towards the lack of cleanliness in the Trans Yamuna localities. Roads and lanes of Gandhi Nagar have become such a casualty of lack of cleanliness that everywhere one can see garbage piled up. The area is in utter neglect now. It has become all the more after the elections got over. Filth and odour fill the locality so much so that the people find it difficult to live healthy. A number of meetings with higher ups brought force no improvement. Failure to take prompt action could result in epidemics spreading its wings. We request health department authorities to step up cleanliness on a war footing.

    Thanking you,

Yours faithfully,
Name

(Sample-15)
Opinion on Rising Prices

Address:
Date:

The Editor
Manthan
Mumbai

Sir,

    I am sending you an opinion price on the relentless price rise for publication in your esteemed newspaper with a view to draw the attention of the government to arrest the price rise. I hope you would spare adequate space in your newspaper.

    Thanking you,

Yours faithfully,
Name

Encl: Opinion price

Relentless Price Rise

A *band* is organised every other day by one political party or another on the closure of factories and companies pushing the general public into unemployment, corruption and black marketing. This has led people to a situation worse than before. It has compelled people to wonder if they would comfortably earn enough to feed their family. The situation becomes worse if you have guests at home, whether its grains vegetables, oil or fruits, the prices have gone through the roof. If consider the plight of a family, where there is just one earning member and three depend including school going children. How would he make both ends meet? Will a middle class family able to survive. Politicians just talk about removing poverty and once in power do things that aggravate the price situation by raising the prices of essential commodities. How will people of this country be able to squarely meet the high prices?

(Sample-16)

Opinion : Today"s Indian Woman is Empowered

Address:

Date:

The Editor
Navbharat Times
Mumbai – 400001

Sir,

    I am sending you an opinion piece, 'Today"s Indian woman is empowered." I hope you will publish this within the 'people"s voice" column.

    Thanking you,

Yours faithfully,

Name

Encl: Opinion piece

Today"s Indian Woman is Empowered

In the Indian society, men and woman are complementary to each other. One doesn"t survive without the other. The Indian society is basically patriarchal. Women and children of the family take the name of the father. There are people who opinion that women don"t have the leadership qualities required to guide the family quietly forgetting that men themselves admit to incompleteness of family without women and that they are the backbone of the family. Today, women are educated, responsible and self-dependent.

They contribute to the family and society, be it being a daughter , sister, mother, statesmen, warriors, physicians, scientists, philosophers, kings and queens – all come out of the wombs God has bestowed woman with. They learn the first lessons of life, speaking, walking, learning, eating food, etc. all in the lap of a woman.

How else would you describe a quality other than as enlightened we all agree that mother, nature has ingrained women with enormous fortitude and patience. It is commonly said that behind every successful man, there is a woman. Now women are breaking all barriers and moving shoulder to shoulder with men folk in all spheres, such as, education, medicine, science, technical education, computer, politics, judiciary, literature, sports, nursing etc. of which primary education and nursing are considered their prerogative. After independence, there has been a phenomenal rise in the enlightenment of women. Mrs. Indira Gandhi led India as the Prime Minister for many years. Mrs. Vijaya Laxmi Pandit became the President of the United Nation"s General Assembly in 1953. Among leading politicians, Sucheta Kriplani, Sushma Swaraj, Sheila Dixit, etc. occupy prime places. Justice Leela Seth of the Delhi High Court became a luminary in her own right.

Who can forget the name of Kalpana Chawla? The first women paratroopers, Geeta Ghosh and aircraft commander Saudamini Deshmukh have glorified Indian women no end. The first woman IPS officer, Kiran Bedi continues to influence women in every field of life. Menfolk have come to accept women as partners in every walk of life.

Women of today have truly become emancipated and enlightened in all respects.

(Sample-17)

[Appeal]

Donation Sought for Treatment

Address:

Date:

The Editor

Yasho Bhumi

Mumbai – 400017

Sir,

    Kindly publish my appeal seeking donation for medical treatment in your esteemed newspaper.

    Thanking you,

Yours faithfully,

Name

Encl: Appeal

Donation for Treatment of Blood Cancer

The 30 year old Dinesh Kumar is a resident of Pant Nagar. He is a renowned sculptor and has been admitted to a hospital in the aftermath of the diagnosis of blood cancer. The doctors attending on him estimate an expense of ₹ 5 lakhs on account of chemotherapy and bone marrow transplantation. Two months back his father expired and there is no one else in the family to raise such a big amount.

    Serving humanity is the highest form of service. We appeal to all the citizens to contribute their might so that the precious life of Dinesh Kumar is saved. Benevolent people may kindly send a cheque or cash to the Cancer Patients Aid Association, Nav Jeevan Memorial Hospital, Samta Uddhyan Pant Nagar-2 (A\C Dinesh Kumar). We would be highly obliged for any kindness.

    Regards,

Name :

Appeal for a Kidney

Address:

Date:

The Editor
Jansatta
Mumbai

Sir,

Kindly publish our humble appeal in your esteemed newspaper.

Thanking you,

Yours faithfully,

Name

Encl: Appeal

Appeal for Donating a Kidney

My father, Suryabhan is being treated at the Deen Dayal Upadhyay Hospital since last month. Doctors have declared both his Kidneys dysfunctional. In this respect, he urgently needs help. We would be grateful from the bottom of our hearts if some benevolent person comes forward and donates one of his kidneys that could save my father"s life. Kind-hearted donors may donate to the Nephrology Department, Deen Dayal Upadhyay Hospital, Delhi.

8 Correspondence with Insurance Companies

Trade and commerce has a close relationship with insurance firms. The insurance of companies protect them against loss, accidental damage, theft, etc. That"s why business houses consider it imperative to insure their assets from any unintended economic loss. Reasons to enter into correspondence with insurance companies may arise on account of the following:

1. Enquiry for insurance of life and property
2. Related to premium
3. Claim against damages

(Sample-1)

Making Enquiry

Ajay Pustak Bhandar

Phone Number

18 Nai Sarak, New Delhi

Date: 28 January, 20XX

The Manager
Oriental Insurance Company
Chandni Chowk,
Delhi

Sir,

I am interested in insuring my shop. Kindly let me have various policies available on this account.

Thanking you,

Yours faithfully,
Ajay Kumar
Proprietor

9
Correspondence with Post Offices

We enter into correspondence with post offices due to a variety of reasons. Sometimes, it becomes necessary to write to them seeking information about the arrival of an important document, non-receipt of a letter, change in address, complaints, resolution or for other commercial reasons. The writer of such letters should come to the point without unnecessary verbosity, while using a polite language.

Samples of correspondence with post offices :

(Sample-1)
Regarding a VPP Sent

Acharya Prakashan
23/1, Main Road, Gandhi Nagar
Delhi – 110031

Telephone:.......   Delhi
Letter No:.........   Dated:.......

The Superintendent of Post Office
11/9, Main Road, Gandhi Nagar
Delhi – 110031

Sir,

We had sent a VPP packet on the 4th of May, 2012 containing books worth ₹ 5,000/- to Pustak Sadan, Bareilly.

The party has informed that the VPP has not reached them till date. Kindly investigate the matter, and help in delivering the same to the addressee.

A photocopy of the postal receipt is enclosed for your necessary action.

Yours faithfully,
Vijay Acharya
Proprietor

(Sample-2)

Seeking a Post Box Number

Acharya Prakashan

Phone No:......   Address:
Ref No:...........   Date:.........

The Superintendent of Post Offices
Head Post Office
Krishna Nagar
Delhi

Sir,

   We want to be allotted a post box number for our official correspondence. Kindly let me know the detail about obtaining one.

   Thanking you,

                                                    Yours faithfully,
                                                    Vijay Acharya
                                                    Proprietor

---

(Sample-3)

Change of Address to the Post Office

Phone No: Address:
Ref. No.   Dated:

The Post Master
Daryaganj
New Delhi

Sir,

   Recently, I have changed my residence and moved into a new house. This new house too falls within the jurisdiction of the Daryaganj Post Office. I have written my old and new address herewith. Henceforth, kindly ensure that all mails are forwarded to this new address.

                                                    Yours faithfully,
                                                    Surendra Kumar

   (Old address)

(Sample-4)

Non-Delivery of Mails in Time

Phone No :   Address:

                                                                                          Date:

The Post Master
GPO
Jhansi

Sir,

It pains me to write that despite many complaints in the past, letters and mails are still not being delivered in time. The new postman assigned for this area delivers mails here and there without caring to deliver at the correct addresses. Often letters are delivered so late that the significance of a letter is lost. I am an insurance agent and on account of late deliveries, I have suffered a loss of around a lakh in the last month only. If things don"t improve, I may have to take the matter to the consumer forum. It is my request to take action immediately to improve the timely deliveries of mails.

Yours faithfully,

Prakash Parmar

10

Job-Related Letters

Job-Related Letters

Every organisation, whether government or non-government run aided by officials and staff, as such, every organisation has to arrange for the engagement of employees. It is done either through calling for applications from prospective, interested persons or on deputation or transfer within the organisation. Persons looking for employment either send in an application mentioning their qualifications or apply in response to vacancies advertised in the newspapers.

Types of Employment Letters

Correspondence with regard to employment begings right from notification of vacancies till the issuance of appointment letters.

- ❑ Notification of vacancies
- ❑ Communicated with media for publicity
- ❑ Receipt of applications
- ❑ Written tests/interviews
- ❑ Verifications of credentials of selected candidates
- ❑ Notification of selected candidates
- ❑ Issuance of appointment letters to selected candidates

Notification Regarding Vacancies

A notification is published once the vacancies and respective qualifications have been decided upon. This has to be done very carefully. The following points must be taken into consideration.

- ❑ Complete address of the organisation
- ❑ Complete details of the department of the issuer of the notification
- ❑ Details of vacancies, such as: number of vacancies, names of the posts and places of postings, etc.
- ❑ Details like formats of applications, etc. methods of sending applications, their last date and addresses, to which they are to be sent.
- ❑ Educational qualifications, experience, reservation, etc. also must be clearly indicated.

(Sample-1)

Wanted

Applications are invited by Career Commerce College Maharana Pratap Nagar, Bhopal for 5 posts of lecturers in commerce. Essential qualification is a first class post-graduate degree in commerce with age, minimum 21 years and the maximum should be 35. Interested candidates may sent their applications latest by the 20th of January, 20XX to Career Commerce College, 24 Maharana Pratap Nagar, Bhopal. Applications received after the last date will not be considered.

Dated
Principal
Career Commerce College
Bhopal

(Sample-2)

Wanted One Office Assistant

Wanted one honest and hard-working assistant for our Delhi Branch. Maximum age 40 years, knowledge of Hindi and English, typing and shorthand is a must, salary as per qualification. Apply with full particulars and send it to Post Box No. 7890, Nariman Point, Mumbai.

Correspondence with Media for the Release of Employment Notification

Government and private business houses use various media outlets, such as newspapers, magazines, radio, TV, etc to inform vacant positions. The first step towards this end which the organisations take recourse to is calling for advertisement tariff cards from the media keeping the importance of the target area and the financial strength of the company. The media selects where vacancies are to be advertised. Following are the samples of correspondence:

(Sample-1)

Jaico Motors
(Leading Distributors of Cars and Two-wheelers)

Telephone No:

34 Moti Nagar, New Delhi
Dated: February 18, 20XX

Ref No: 2012/Advt/135

The Advertisement Manager
Navbharat Times
7, Bahadur Shah Zafar Marg
New Delhi

Sub: Advertisement Tariff

Sir,

From time to time, we release advertisements and other important circulars for publication in various newspapers. We request you to kindly send us a copy of your advertisement tariff for our consideration. We would appreciate if you include the tariff for special supplements also.

Thanking you,

Yours faithfully,
Neeraj Saraswati
Manager

(Sample-2)

Arti Vastralaya
(Saree Manufacturer and Distributor)

Telephone No:

Address:
Date:

Ref No:

The Director
Doordarshan Kendra
Vadodara (Gujarat)

Sub: Advertisement Tariff

Sir,

We are interested in releasing advertisement of our colourful sarees on various regional channels as also on the National Channel No-1 of the Doordarshan. In this regard, kindly send us your latest advertisement tariff list to enable us to decide on the channels we wish to release advertisements.

Thanking you,

Yours faithfully,
Dherendra Bhatia
Manager

Requested Letters/ Cover Letters

Request letters represent our identifications and credentials. They draw attention of the receiver to think about ourselves, give consideration to why a particular group of letters have been written, their purposes etc.

Request/Cover Letters and their types:

- ❑ Employment-related letters
- ❑ Admission-related
- ❑ Convenience-related
- ❑ Material-related
- ❑ Permission-related
- ❑ Issuance of certificates
- ❑ For proper and fair decisions

Employment-related

An application sent for seeking job is known as an application-related to employment. Such letters are written based on the information gathered through the newspapers. While writing an application to an employer, the source of information must be identified.

Salient Points while Writing an Application

- ❑ Application must be written on a plain white sheet
- ❑ Typed briefly and to the point
- ❑ Use one side of the paper only
- ❑ There should be margins on all four sides
- ❑ Complete address of the sender should be mentioned
- ❑ Abbreviations should not be used
- ❑ Should be free of grammatical errors
- ❑ Highlight the important milestones of your career
- ❑ Carbon copy must never be sent
- ❑ All documents asked for in the advertisements must be attached
- ❑ Qualifications and references should not be unduly highlighted
- ❑ If Postal Order/DD is to be attached, your name and address should be written on the back.
- ❑ If photo is also enclosed, it must bear the applicant"s name and address
- ❑ Original documents should not be enclosed
- ❑ If one is applying for a job, while being in employment, then please send the advance copy to the prospective employer and another copy through your current employer, if required.

(Sample-1)

Application for the Post of Salesman

The Rangarang Vastra Nirmata
45, Rajwada
Indore

Sub: Application for the Post of a Sales Executive

Dear Sir,

I have reliably learnt that you are looking for a sales executive at your Bhopal branch to promote and sale 'Rangarang Sarees" manufactured by you. I have got 5 years of experience in this trade. I am offering my candidature for the above post. My particulars are as under:

Name	:	Nirbhay Singh
Address	:	House Address
Experience:	1.	Rajesh Vastralaya Indore as Sales Representative for Sarees from…….to………..
	2.	Rajkumar Silk Mills Surat as Sales Representative for Sarees from……………to………………

I hope you will give me an opportunity to prove my worth.

Thanking you,

Date:........

Yours faithfully,
Nirbhay Singh

Encl:

1. Rajesh Vastralaya – Photocopy of experience certificate
2. Rajkumar Silk Mills – photocopy of commendation certificate

(Sample-2)

Application for the Post of an Accountant

The K. P. Publishers
26/2, Daryaganj
New Delhi

Sub–Application for the Post of an Accountant

Sir,

With reference to your advertisement in the *Dainik Samachar* dated 1st January, 20XX for the post of Accountants, I am sending my particulars and offering my candidature for the same.

Name	:	Gaurav Gupta
Father"s Name	:	Sh. Dheeraj Gupta
Address	:	120, Archana Apartment
		Paschim Vihar
		New Delhi-110063
Date of Birth	:	20th November, 1980
Educational Qualification	:	1. B.Com, Delhi University
		2. M.Com, Delhi University
Experience	:	Worked as an Accountant with Rahat Book Stall, Sarojini Nagar
		New Delhi from ………………..to …………………

With regards to my qualifications and experience, I hope you will offer me a chance to prove my worth.

Thanking you,

Yours faithfully,
Gaurav Gupta

Date:………..

Encl: 1. Photocopies of Mark Sheets of B.Com & M.Com

2. Photocopy of experience certificate from Rahat Book Stall

Written Examination/Interview – Notification

Application of candidates for different posts are checked and processed as per the eligibility criteria and those found suitable are asked to report for written exam and/or interview as the case may be. If the number of applicants is not large, direct interviews are conducted in normal course. Otherwise written exams of eligible candidates take place first and those found suitable are called for interview at a later date. Following are some of the examples of written and interview letters:

(Sample-1)

Anmol Vastra Bhandar
(Modern Clothing and Saree Manufacturer)
45, Chandni Chowk, Delhi

Telephone: E-mail:
Ref: Interview/2012/15

Subject – Interview

Dear Mr. Ravi Tiwari,

With reference to your application dated...........for the post of Sales Representative (Saree) for our Moradabad branch, please report at the above address at 12 noon on dated......... You must carry the recommendatory letters from two respectable business houses.

Thanking you,

Rupesh Kumar
Anmol Vastra Bhandar
Delhi

**Office of the Principal, Government College
Dewas (Madhya Pradesh)**

Ref No: Interview/2012/134   Dewas, February 2, 20XX

Sri Akhilesh Tripathi
56 Sethi Nagar
Ujjain

Sub: Written Examination & Interview

With reference to your application dated........for the post of Lecturer in English, please be informed that the written exam and interview has been scheduled as below. Please carry all your original certificates and a photocopy of each, while reporting here. No TA/DA is admissible to the candidates.

Lecturer (English) – written exam and interview

Written exam – 3rd March, 20XX, Time: 10 am to 12 noon

Interview – 3rd March, 20XX, Time: 2 pm onwards

Principal
Government College
Dewas

Verification of Credentials of the Selected Candidates

The documents submitted by the selected candidates are put through a verification process to ascertain their correctness and authenticity. Background checks are also made to establish that the candidates so selected are trustworthy. Correspondence with their previous employees are made to establish their efficiency, group behaviour productivity, etc. Some examples are given below:

(Sample-1)

Enquiry Regarding Credentials

Raghu Kitchen Bartan Bhandar
(Deals in Kitchen Utensils)

Telephone No: 20 Patni Bazaar, Ujjain
                                                               Date: April 2, 2012
Ref No:

Sri Ganesh Bhandar
Madhav Nagar
Indore

Sub: Regarding Sri Pradeep Sharma

Dear Sir,

Mr. Pradeep Sharma has applied for the post of salesman. We have learnt from his application that he had worked in your shop sometime back. We would be glad to have your feedback regarding his reliability and trustworthiness. Please be assured that any information supplied by you would be kept private and confidential. We hope no inconvenience is caused to you in this regard.

Yours faithfully,
Raghuvansh Singh
For Raghu Kitchen Bartan Bhandar

(Sample-2)

Verification of Credentials

Shiksha Prakashan, Indore
Sadar Bazaar, Indore

Telephone No: 23, Sadar Bazaar, Indore
Ref No: 183   Date: May 5, 2012

M/S Rama Book Depot
Nai Sarak
Khandawa (M.P)

Dear Sir,

Sri Sachin Verma has applied for the post of Accountant with us. He has mentioned your name in the reference column. We would be glad to receive your feedback regarding the suitability or otherwise of his candidature. We would appreciate an early reply.

Thanking you,

Yours faithfully,
Viren Saxena
Shiksha Prakashan
Indore

Informing the Candidate of his Selection

After written examinations, interviews and background checks, the selection committee is convinced of the suitability of the candidate in all respects. Hence, the candidate is informed accordingly that he/she has been selected for the post. The candidate is then given an appointment letter. If this is not received by a particular date, he/she may directly report at the address mentioned below:

(Address is mentioned here)

Saraswati Publishing House
Nai Sarak, Delhi

Telephone No: Delhi, Date: June 12, 20XX

Sri Satyanarayan Sharma
Daryaganj, Delhi

Dear Sir,

With reference to your application dated………….., we are pleased to inform you that your name has been recommended for selection as a Branch Manager of our new branch at Kalyan, Mumbai. The appointment letter would be mailed to you by the end of this month.

Thanking you,

Suresh Sharma
Saraswati Publishing House
Delhi

Appointment Letter

An appointment letter is one that informs the selected person about his selection for a particular post at the designated office. Terms and conditions of appointment may also be indicated therein.

Contents of an Appointment Letter

- ❑ Address of the appointing office
- ❑ Name of the appointed person
- ❑ Designation of the person appointed
- ❑ Salary allowances and other perquisites
- ❑ Terms of appointment
- ❑ Date of appointment
- ❑ Duration of appointment
- ❑ Type of appointment – permanent, temporary or probation
- ❑ Date of joining
- ❑ Place of joining

(Sample-1)

Office of the Principal, Government College, Sagar (M.P)

Ref No: App/2012/16   Sagar, Date: June 23, 20XX

Appointment Letter

Sri Ajay Aggarwal is hereby appointed as an Assistant in this office. The salary payable is in the ₹ 10,000 – ₹ 15000/- grade. Please join your duty within 14 days from the date of issuance of this letter. You would be on probation for a period of one year.

Signature
Principal
Government College, Sagar

(Sample-2)

Arya Prakashan
55, Hawa Mahal Road, Jaipur

Telephone No: Jaipur, Date:
Ref: No:

Sri Akash Sharma
15, Naya Bazaar
Jaipur

Sir,

You are hereby appointed as a Sales Representative in our firm. You will be paid a consolidated salary of ₹ 10,000/- per month. Your employment would remain effective for one year from the date of your joining. Failure to join the duty before may entail cancellation of your appointment.

Signature
Aseem Rathi
Manager
Arya Prakashan

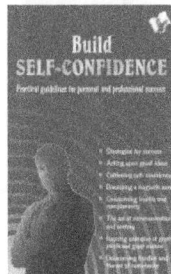

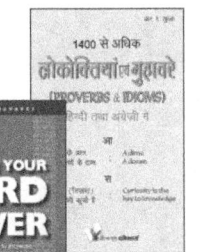

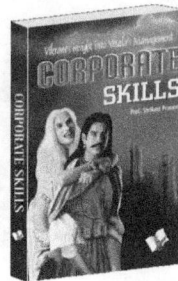

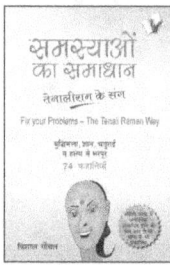

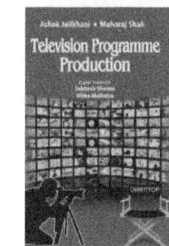

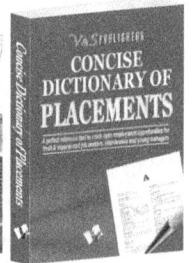

STUDENT DEVELOPMENT/LEARNING
(छात्र विकास/लर्निंग)

JOKES
(हास्य)

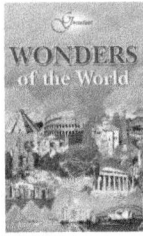

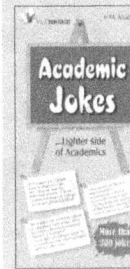

MAGIC & FACT (जादू एवं तथ्य)

MUSIC (संगीत)

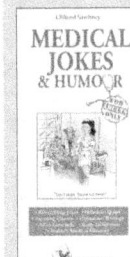

COMPUTER

Quiz Books
(प्रश्नोत्तरी की पुस्तकें)

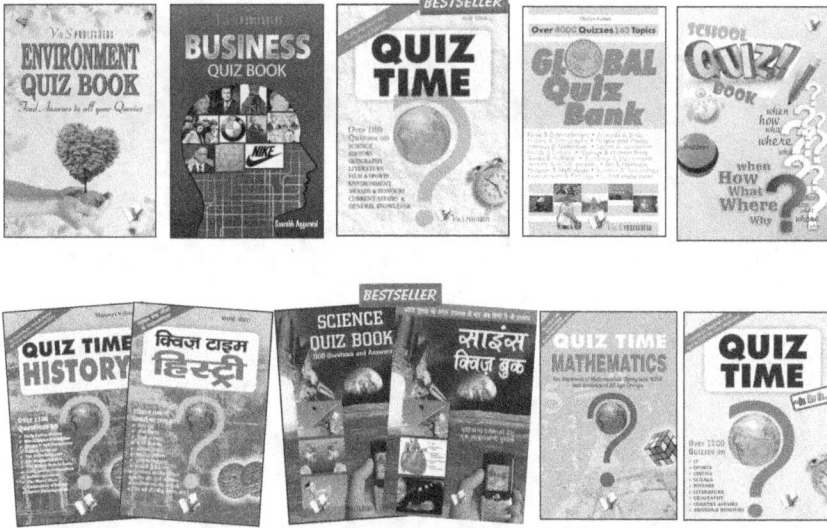

- ENVIRONMENT QUIZ BOOK
- BUSINESS QUIZ BOOK
- QUIZ TIME
- GLOBAL Quiz Bank
- SCHOOL QUIZ BOOK
- QUIZ TIME HISTORY
- क्विज़ टाइम हिस्ट्री
- SCIENCE QUIZ BOOK
- साईंस क्विज़ बुक
- QUIZ TIME MATHEMATICS
- QUIZ TIME

MYSTERIES
(रहस्य)

- World Famous UNSOLVED MYSTERIES
- विश्व-प्रसिद्ध अनसुलझे रहस्य
- भूत-प्रेत घटनाएं
- UFO CASE FILES

DRAWING BOOKS (ड्राइंग बुक्स)

- ड्राइंग एण्ड पेंटिंग कोर्स
- Drawing & Painting Course
- ड्राइंग कार्टून्स
- DRAWING CARTOONS
- Drawing & Painting Course Volume II

QUOTES/SAYINGS (उद्धरण/सूक्तिवर्णी)

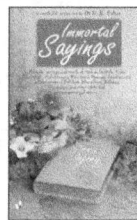

- Inspirational Quotes and Thoughts
- प्रेरक सूक्ति कोष
- Immortal Sayings

BIOGRAPHIES (आत्म कथाएँ)

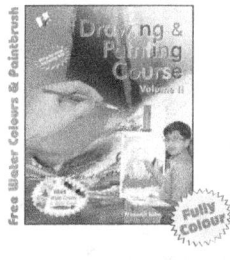

- GREAT PERSONALITIES OF THE WORLD
- FAMOUS INDIANS OF THE 20TH CENTURY
- Nobel Peace Prize Winners

PUZZLES (पहेलियाँ)

- MATHEMAGIC Puzzles & Brain Drainers
- SUDOKU
- SUDOKU
- SUDOKU NEW
- Mind Benders Brain Teasers

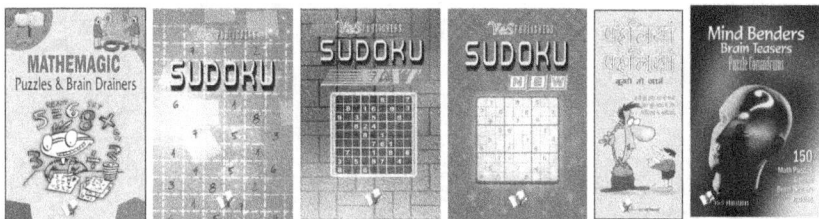

ACTIVITIES BOOK (एक्टिविटीज बुक)

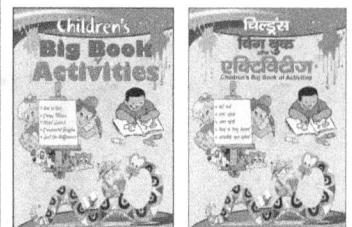

- Children's Big Book Activities
- चिल्ड्रंस बिग बुक एक्टिविटीज

CHILDREN'S ENCYCLOPEDIA
THE WORLD OF KNOWLEDGE

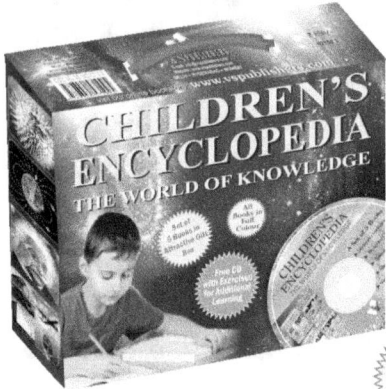

All Books in Full Colour

Free CD for additional reference

Set of 5 Books in Attractive Gift Box

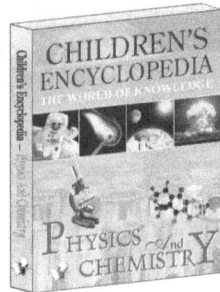

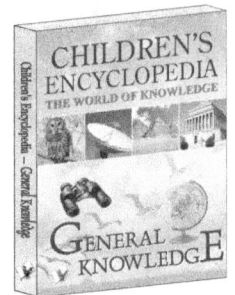

Code: 02152 S

CHILDREN'S ENCYCLOPEDIA — THE WORLD OF KNOWLEDGE — LIFE SCIENCES and HUMAN BODY

CHILDREN'S ENCYCLOPEDIA — THE WORLD OF KNOWLEDGE — PHYSICS and CHEMISTRY

CHILDREN'S ENCYCLOPEDIA — THE WORLD OF KNOWLEDGE — SPACE SCIENCE and ELECTRONICS

CHILDREN'S ENCYCLOPEDIA — THE WORLD OF KNOWLEDGE — SCIENTISTS INVENTIONS and DISCOVERIES

CHILDREN'S ENCYCLOPEDIA — THE WORLD OF KNOWLEDGE — GENERAL KNOWLEDGE

71 SERIES (71 श्रृंखला)

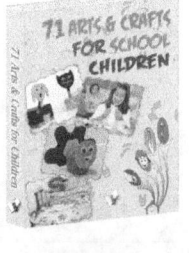

71 +10 New Mathematics Projects — Free Interactive CD

Spice in Science — The best of Science funnies

71 साइंस प्रोजेक्ट्स

71 +10 New Science Projects — Self-learning Kit

71 +10 புதிய அறிவியல் திட்டங்கள் — Self-learning Kit

71 +10 ...

71 Electrical & Electronic Projects — For Beginners, Intermediate, and Engineering Students

71 Famous Scientists — Coming Soon

71 साइंस एक्सपेरिमेंट्स

71 Science Experiments

71 +10 New Science Projects Junior

71 +10 साइंस प्रोजेक्ट्स जूनियर

Greatest Scientists of the World — Coming Soon

WORLD-FAMOUS Scientists

71 +10 Science Activities

71 +10 साइंस एक्टिविटीज

71 +10 Magic Tricks for Children

71 ARTS & CRAFTS FOR SCHOOL CHILDREN

www.ingramcontent.com/pod-product-compliance
Lightning Source LLC
LaVergne TN
LVHW081328060426
835513LV00012B/1229